BE
FOUNDATION

Be Good. Be Kind. Be Love.

In honor of

Elleana + Isabella Gaddis

befoundation.info

THE BANTAM LIBRARY
of Culinary Arts

Pasta

JILL NORMAN

BANTAM BOOKS

TORONTO · NEW YORK · LONDON · SYDNEY · AUCKLAND

A DORLING KINDERSLEY BOOK

PASTA

A BANTAM BOOK/PUBLISHED BY ARRANGEMENT WITH
DORLING KINDERSLEY LIMITED

PRINTING HISTORY
DORLING KINDERSLEY EDITION
PUBLISHED IN GREAT BRITAIN IN 1990

BANTAM EDITION/MAY 1991

EDITOR LAURA HARPER
SENIOR EDITOR CAROLYN RYDEN
AMERICAN EDITOR BECKY CABAZA
DESIGN MATHEWSON BULL
PHOTOGRAPHER DAVE KING

Every effort has been made to provide accurate conversions from metric to American measures,
though some ingredient amounts have been rounded off to the closest American measure.

LIBRARY OF CONGRESS CATALOGING-IN-PUBLICATION DATA

NORMAN, JILL.
PASTA/JILL NORMAN.
P. CM. – (THE BANTAM LIBRARY OF CULINARY ARTS)
INCLUDES INDEX.
1. COOKERY (PASTA) 2. PASTA.
I. TITLE. II. SERIES.
TX809.M17N648 1991
841.8'22–DC20
90-40241 CIP
ISBN 0-553-07221-8

BANTAM BOOKS ARE PUBLISHED BY BANTAM BOOKS, A DIVISION OF BANTAM
DOUBLEDAY DELL PUBLISHING GROUP, INC. ITS TRADEMARK, CONSISTING OF THE
WORDS "BANTAM BOOKS" AND THE PORTRAYAL OF A ROOSTER, IS REGISTERED IN
U.S. PATENT AND TRADEMARK OFFICE AND IN OTHER COUNTRIES. MARCA
REGISTRADA. BANTAM BOOKS, 666 FIFTH AVENUE, NEW YORK, NEW YORK 10103.

PRINTED AND BOUND IN HONG KONG BY IMAGO
0 9 8 7 6 5 4 3 2 1

C O N T E N T S

INTRODUCTION

$\mathscr{P}$ASTA AND NOODLES – *the name varies with the country of origin – are made from flour mixed with a liquid, usually egg or water. Flavorings or colorings, such as spinach, herbs, tomato purée, olives, or cuttlefish ink, are sometimes added to the basic dough. This is kneaded, rolled, cut, perhaps stuffed, then boiled, steamed, baked, or fried, and served with a sauce or in a broth.*

Pasta has its roots in many cultures. The Etruscans and ancient Greeks ate pasta and had special implements to shape it; Apicius, the Roman gourmet, included it in his De Re Coquinaria (On Cookery). *Several centuries later the Arabs took pasta from the eastern Mediterranean to Spain.*

Long before Marco Polo made his journey across Asia, noodles were a staple of the diet there. They were street food, the basic everyday food of the poor, but also appeared at banquets as a symbol of longevity. As the Mongols moved west in the 13th century they took their stuffed pasta and small dumplings across Siberia.

The stuffed pasta of Asia and Europe is all made in a similar way. Triangles, crescents, squares, and circles are filled with a variety of foods and then fried, baked, or boiled.

Chinese wontons, *filled with pork or shrimp, are served in a broth or deep-fried as a snack. Mongol* pel'meni *spread west from Siberia and today are popular everywhere in the Soviet Union. In the Ukraine they are called* vareniki; *in Armenia (and Turkey)* mantı. *The* kreplachs *of the central European Jews are closely related to* pel' meni, *and to the* pierogi *of Polish cooking. They are served in soup or fried in chicken fat to accompany a meat dish.*

Undeniably the Italians have the greatest variety of all forms of pasta and even more names. In the 14th century Francesco Datini, the Merchant of Prato, wrote in his private papers of ravioli being served as a delicacy at the first course of a banquet. They were stuffed with ground pork, eggs, cheese, a little sugar, and parsley,

Italian pasta label

then fried and served powdered with sugar. Bartolomeo Scappi's great cookery book of 1570 has recipes for tagliatelle and maccheroni cooked in broth or milk and served with cinnamon and sugar. By this time pasta was available commercially, but was expensive. The guild of pasta makers, the vermicellai, now demanded the sole right to make pasta and guarded their trade jealously from the bakers. Pasta shops proliferated throughout Italy. By 1785 there were 280 in Naples; the streets were full of racks of pasta drying in the hot wind, and of maccheroni sellers cooking on street corners. By the 19th century Naples had a huge pasta industry, and the thousands of emigrants who sailed for the United States took their staple food with them, thus ensuring its continued popularity across the Atlantic.

FRESH PASTA

*I*T IS QUITE EASY *to make fresh pasta at home – see p. 24 – and well worth the effort. The basic form for every variety is the* sfoglia, *a sheet of dough, which is cut to ribbons of varying width, or into the large squares or rounds used for filled pasta.*

see p. 24

Common dried pasta shapes
come in several colors, but the
black pasta made with the ink of
cuttlefish is only obtainable fresh.

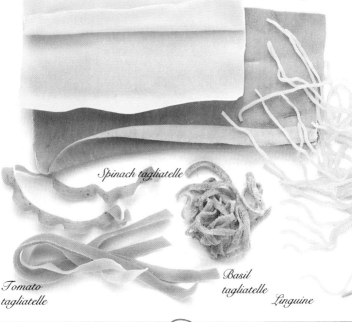

*Lasagne and
lasagne verdi*

Spinach tagliatelle

*Tomato
tagliatelle*

*Basil
tagliatelle*

Linguine

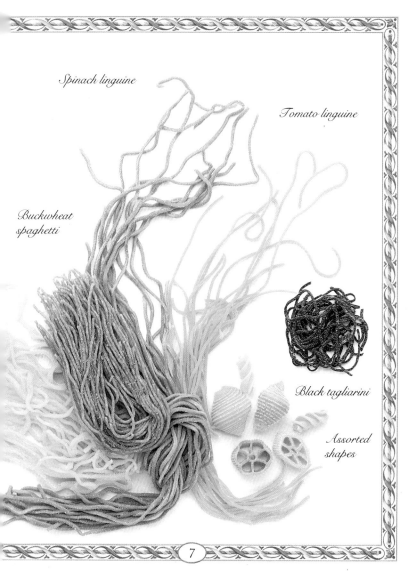

Spinach linguine

Tomato linguine

Buckwheat
spaghetti

Black tagliarini

Assorted
shapes

7

RIBBONS & STICKS

*F*LAT PASTA *is usually made with egg. Under American food law, the definition of any commercial product called noodles specifies the use of egg. Fresh egg pasta is lighter and more delicate than the dried version, and amply repays the effort of making it at home (see the instructions on p. 24). A flat sheet of dough is cut into the required shapes: wide for lasagne, ribbons for fettuccine and tagliatelle, and fine strands for linguine.*

Lasagne and lasagne verdi

Whole wheat spaghetti is an invention of health food commercialism, not much favored in Italy where everybody knows that pasta is neither fattening nor likely to cause any other problems.

Spaghetti

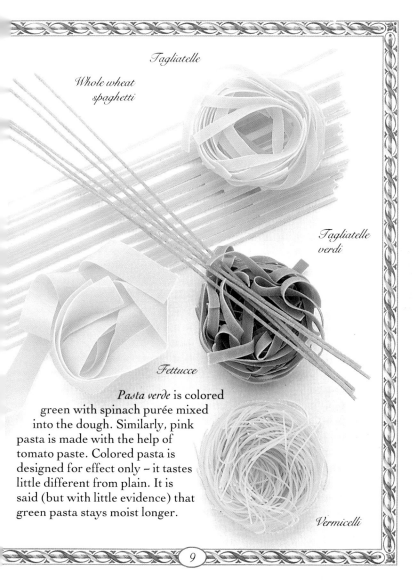

Tagliatelle

Whole wheat spaghetti

Tagliatelle verdi

Fettucce

Pasta verde is colored green with spinach purée mixed into the dough. Similarly, pink pasta is made with the help of tomato paste. Colored pasta is designed for effect only – it tastes little different from plain. It is said (but with little evidence) that green pasta stays moist longer.

Vermicelli

TUBES

*T*HE TWO PRINCIPAL *ways of cooking pasta are boiling or baking. Baked pasta* (pasta al forno) *is usually made either with large flat sheets of egg pasta* (lasagne) *alternating with a thick sauce of vegetables or meat, or by stuffing one of the tubular shapes* (tufoli, rigatoni, *and the most famous of them all,* cannelloni)*. The stuffed shapes are then covered with more of the sauce, or with a different sauce, and baked in the oven. Smaller tubes may be baked in a sauce as a gratin.*

Rigatoni

Elbow macaroni

Most dried pasta shapes are made of a very hard grain called durum wheat, ground to an amber flour called *semola* or *semolina* in Italian, which can be confusing in English: be sure to ask for *semolina flour*, not just *semolina*. Fresh pasta can be made with bread flour or with regular unbleached flour.

Maccheroncelli

Ziti (bridegrooms)

Penne (quills)

Cannelloni

Occhi di lupo
(wolf's eyes)

SMALL SHAPES

*T*HERE IS AN ENDLESS VARIETY *of very small shapes of pasta, collectively known as* pastina, *ranging from solid little blobs called* orzo *(barley) or* semi *(seeds) to more fanciful miniature shapes. These are given to children or used in light broths topped with a little grated cheese.*

Funghini

Anellini rigati

Animal shape

Soups destined to serve as a main course, such as min-estrone or pasta e fagioli, do not rely on these small shapes for their pasta content but use some of the larger forms, from elbow macaroni to the finger-long and finger-thick pizzoccheri of the Valtellina. Stuffed pasta, too, is used in broth.

Fiochetti

Stellini

Conchigliette piccole

SHELLS & TWISTS

*I*TALIAN PASTA *comes in a bewildering variety of shapes, whereas in middle Europe – from southern Germany and Switzerland to the Balkan countries – only the flat varieties we call noodles and small soup pieces are traditional. Apart from the patterns dictated by finger movements, shapes have proliferated with the increase of commercial die-stamping.*

The many corkscrew shapes, which in the home are made by twirling pasta around a knitting needle, or folding a strand in the middle and twisting it around itself (*gemelli*, twins), are particularly effective to hold cheese and other sticky sauces.

Conchigliette

Conchiglie

Gnocchi

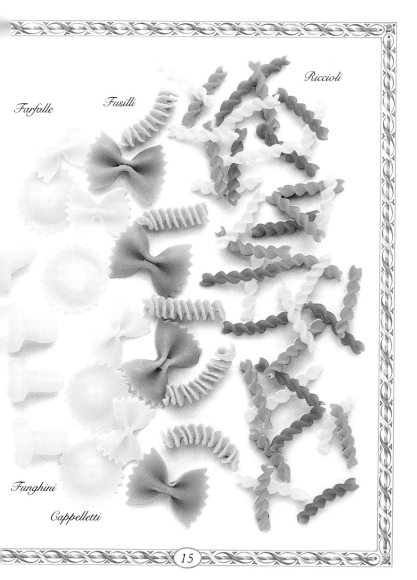

Farfalle

Fusilli

Riccioli

Funghini

Cappelletti

ITALIAN
STUFFED
PASTA

Tortellini

*S*TUFFED PASTA (pasta
ripiena) *is always much better
fresh than store-bought. It is made in many
shapes and sizes, with a great variety of
regional names – those above right are
tortellini, or twists. There is no such thing
as a traditional stuffing for any one shape,
but Italian fillings tend to be savory,
whether using leftovers or resulting
from pure fancy.*

Cappelletti

The round shapes sealed
with a "brim" of dough
are usually called *cappelletti*
(little hats) or *capelli
di prete* (priests' hats).
The larger variety
of *capelli* is also
called *orecchioni*
(large ears). Many
of the pasta names
describe a basic shape.
A variant, circular form of
tortellini is made, like
ravioli, from two pieces of
sfoglia rather than by
folding one piece in half.

Orecchioni

*Round
tortelloni*

Small ravioli

Ravioli

As *tortelloni* are associated with Bologna and *cappelletti* with the central provinces in general, so ravioli are traditionally thought of as Genovese. The smaller ravioli often contain pork and beef, while larger ones have spinach and ricotta.

Agnolotti, from Piedmont, have a larger pasta edge than ravioli. They are made from a single piece of *sfoglia* folded over the filling.

Agnolotti

Square tortelloni

ORIENTAL PASTA

ALL OF ASIA eats noodles. In the north they are usually made with wheat flour, while in the south rice flour predominates. There are also noodles made from mung bean starch, which have different properties: when deep-fried, they puff up and become crunchy; when soaked, they have a spongelike capacity to absorb any sauce.

Illustrated below are rice sticks and rice noodles. Rice sticks will break into short lengths when cooked; they can also be fried like bean threads. Rice noodles are best when fresh: the packet they come in should be supple. On the far right are two types of Chinese egg noodles. One is crinkly, the other plain. On the near right are three kinds of thin noodles or *vermicelli*: at the top, two parcels of rice noodles; below those is a bundle of bean starch noodles that need only be soaked, but can then withstand up to 20 minutes of braising without losing shape or texture; in the middle is a bundle of Japanese *somen*, a wheat flour noodle cooked while tied up, and eaten cold.

Rice sticks

Rice noodles

Rice
noodles

Bean starch noodles

Crinkly egg noodles

Egg noodles

Somen

19

PASTA FROM CENTRAL & EASTERN EUROPE

*R*USSIA, POLAND, HUNGARY, *and the
Balkan countries use noodles, stuffed
pasta, and dumplings – either boiled or deep-fried
– as staple foods. The Asian and Turkish inva-
sions brought in dessert varieties with fruit, jam,
or other sweet fillings. Irregular pieces, grated from hard balls
of egg-and-flour dough (above right) are known by various
names:* Spätzle *in German,* tarhonya *in Hungarian,
and* zacierki *in Polish.*

Spätzle

The shapes of stuffed pasta are variants on folding
a round or square piece of the basic sheet.
Traditional Jewish *kreplach* (shown here,
with the chicken liver filling of p. 35)
is a square folded diagonally; the
half-moon *pierogi* (on the opposite
page) start as circles. Thimble
dumplings (top right,
opposite) are made
from a double layer
of dough, and
puff into balls
when fried.

Kreplach

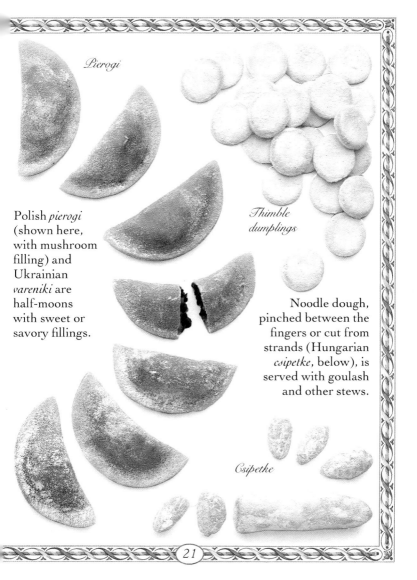

Pierogi

Thimble dumplings

Polish *pierogi* (shown here, with mushroom filling) and Ukrainian *vareniki* are half-moons with sweet or savory fillings.

Noodle dough, pinched between the fingers or cut from strands (Hungarian *csipetke*, below), is served with goulash and other stews.

Csipetke

PASTA PARCELS

$\mathscr{T}$HE DOUGH *for stuffed pasta has a flour, egg, and water base, and it is often used both for a dumpling version and for "skins" to wrap around different fillings. The resulting parcels can be either boiled or deep-fried. Boiling is done in water if the pasta is to accompany a dish, or in stock that will be served with the pasta.*

Vareniki

Manti

Manti are a Turkish and Armenian dish. They usually have a filling of ground meat with very subtle spicing – a recipe can be found on p. 38.

Vareniki are a specialty of the Ukraine. Their filling follows the seasons: cherries, berries, mushrooms, sauerkraut, and preserves are used.

The fillings for these pasta parcels vary enormously according to what is locally available – seafood, meat, cheese, and fruit are among the staple ingredients. The savory versions are often served as snacks, or sold as street food, while sweet or fruit-filled varieties usually make a dessert. Meat-, cheese-, and vegetable-filled parcels also go into stews.

Pel'meni

Wontons

Pel'meni from Siberia (served with a mustard and vinegar sauce there, a filling of greens in Central Asia) are sold throughout Russia in special cafés, *pel'mennaya*.

Wontons, common throughout China as deep-fried snacks (savory, with a dip, or fruit-filled and sugared), are better known to us in soup.

Recipes

All recipes are for 4
as a main course or for
6 as a starter

FRESH PASTA

The basic proportions for making fresh pasta are ³/₄ cup/ 100 g flour to 1 egg, but the exact amount will vary according to the flour and the freshness and size of the eggs. Commercial pasta is made with flour from durum wheat, an extremely hard flour that has a high gluten content and requires a lot of kneading. Bread flour combined with regular unbleached flour is best for homemade pasta.

1¹/₈ cups/150 g bread flour
1¹/₈ cups/150 g flour
salt
3 eggs

Mix together the two flours with a good pinch of salt and make a mound on a clean work surface. Make a well in the middle and break in the eggs. Beat the eggs